Symbols of the United States

Sarah Machajewski

ROSEN
COMMON CORE
READERS

New York

Published in 2013 by The Rosen Publishing Group, Inc.
29 East 21st Street, New York, NY 10010

Book Design: Katelyn Londino

Photo Credits: Cover Gary Blakeley/Shutterstock.com; p. 4 Dmitriy Shironosov/Shutterstock.com; p. 5 fstockfoto/Shutterstock.com; p. 6 Shipov Oleg/Shutterstock.com; pp. 7, 22 (eagle) Natalia Lysenko/Shutterstock.com; p. 8 Mark Gibson/Photolibrary/Getty Images; pp. 9, 22 (Liberty Bell) Racheal Grazias/Shutterstock.com; p. 10 JOSEPH NETTIS/Photo Researchers/Getty Images; pp. 11, 23 (Paul Revere statue) Jorge Salcedo/Shutterstock.com; p. 12 Christopher Parpa/Shutterstock.com; pp. 13, 22 (Statue of Liberty) Amy Nichole Harris/Shutterstock.com; pp. 14, 22, 23 (Mount Rushmore) gary yim/Shutterstock.com; p. 15 Boykov/Shutterstock.com; p. 16 Chung Sung-Jun/Staff/Getty Images News/Getty Images; pp. 17, 20, 22 (flag, Uncle Sam), 23 (Uncle Sam) JustASC/Shutterstock.com; pp. 18, 23 (American flag) Alessandro Campagnolo/Shutterstock.com; p. 19 stockstudios/Shutterstock.com; p. 21 Andersen Ross/Stockbyte/Getty Images.

ISBN: 978-1-4488-8761-3
6-pack ISBN: 978-1-4488-8762-0

Manufactured in the United States of America

CPSIA Compliance Information: Batch #WS12RC: For further information contact Rosen Publishing, New York, New York at 1-800-237-9932.

Word Count: 194

Contents

I live in the United States.

My country has many symbols.

A symbol is an object
that stands for something else.

One symbol is the bald eagle.
Bald eagles fly in the sky.

They're big, strong birds.
America is big and strong, too.

The Liberty Bell is a symbol.
Liberty means that you are free.

Being free means that nobody can tell you how to live.

All Americans are free.

That's what the Liberty Bell stands for.

America has many symbols that are statues.
Statues look like people or animals.

The Statue of Liberty welcomes people to the United States.

She shows people
that Americans are free.

Another symbol is Mount Rushmore.
It's on a mountain.

Mount Rushmore has four faces on it.
Do you know who they are?

Our flag is red, white, and blue.
It has stars and stripes.

The stars stand for the number of states in America.

People love the American flag.
It stands for my country.

Another symbol is Uncle Sam.
He is tall and has a white beard.

Uncle Sam wears red, white, and blue.
He loves America.

These symbols are important.
They teach me about my country!

American Symbols

Liberty Bell

the bald eagle

Mount Rushmore

Statue of Liberty

Uncle Sam

American flag

Words to Know

beard

flag

mountain

statue

Index